How Til Spake Ulster

A Beginners Guide
to the Language Spoken
in the North of Ireland

Doreen McBride

ADARE PRESS
White Gables
Ballymoney Hill
Banbridge
Telephone: (018206) 23782

Published by Adare Press
Typeset by December Publications
Printed by Banbridge Chronicle

Introduction

Kelly's World Language Institute awarded me an honorary degree for my services in writing a best selling text-book, *'Speakin' Norn Iron As She Shud Be Spoke'*, which had the express purpose of helping foreigners become conversant with the beautiful language spoken in the North of Ireland, also called Ulster, and locally known as Norn Iron.

I am grateful for the honour conferred and the rights awarded, namely, to maintain a fleet of longships on Lough Neagh for pillaging purposes and to drive my flock of geese across the bridge at Toome without paying tribute. At my graduation ceremony Professor Owen Kelly, the founder of the Institute congratulated me on my achievement in furthering the science of nonsense, then suggested that my work was too advanced for beginners. He said, and on reflection I agree wholeheartedly with him, that it is necessary to be either a native or to spend years in academic study in such places as pubs and maternity clinics, to realise that the North of Ireland is known locally as NORN IRON and that in the same way as the English speak English, the French speak French, Italians Italian, and so on, natives of Norn Iron speak their own language called Norn Ironspeak, or Ulster.

Professor Kelly suggested the production of a beginners guide to the language, something simple and well illustrated, suitable for a generation of couch potatoes who sit night after night glued to television, exhausted by the stress of modern living, worn out by the words written on forms designed by bureaucrats, unable to concentrate long enough to assimilate a page of print. As someone who has always been a Philistine I am delighted to cater for the millions, who seem to have joined me since the advent of Thatcherism.

I respectfully dedicate this book to my cousin Christine Picken and her husband Bobby, in memory of a hilarious Christmas spent in Toronto drinking and recalling the rich language of our youth, to Owen Kelly, who provided the inspiration for this unacademic work and to Maeve Binchy whose aptitude with words I envy. She is a wonderful person, able to inspire even Philistines to take readily to the written page.

How to use this book

The language of Ulster (Norn Iron) is extremely complex. Any basic concept in English will have many Ulster equivalents because the natives, in common with all Irish people, are in love with words. Fluent speakers of Ulster utter a rich flow of language making it essential for serious students to do likewise and learn many ways of expressing concepts.

Knowledge is gained through both the eye and the ear so as an aid to learning this book contains two parts.

Part 1. Illustrated Basic Vocabulary

This section is essentially 'look and say'. It contains simple everyday concepts such as 'I am hungry', accompanied by a cartoon as an aid to memory. Look at the cartoon and the concept, then practise the Ulster translation aloud. It is important to remember that one way of saying something is not sufficient, not if the aim is either to sound like a native or to understand native speech.

Part 2. Additional Vocabulary

It is important to master the vocabulary of Part 1, before attempting this section.

Subject *Page*

Me, Myself

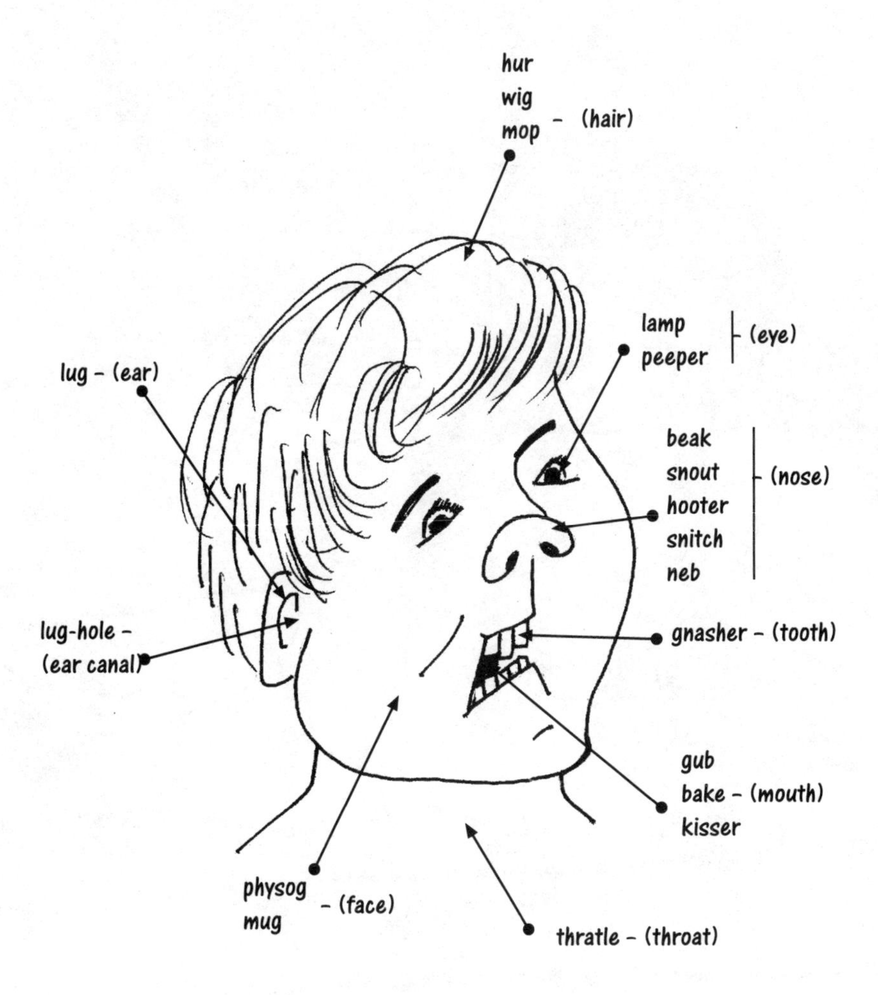
hur
wig
mop - (hair)
lamp
peeper - (eye)
lug - (ear)
beak
snout
hooter
snitch
neb - (nose)
lug-hole -
(ear canal)
gnasher - (tooth)
gub
bake - (mouth)
kisser
physog
mug - (face)
thratle - (throat)

I Feel Tired

Ah'm snookered
Ah'm banjaxed
Ah'm poleaxed
Ah could go out laike a light
Ah'm crocked

My feet are hurting me

I feel very well

I do not feel well at all

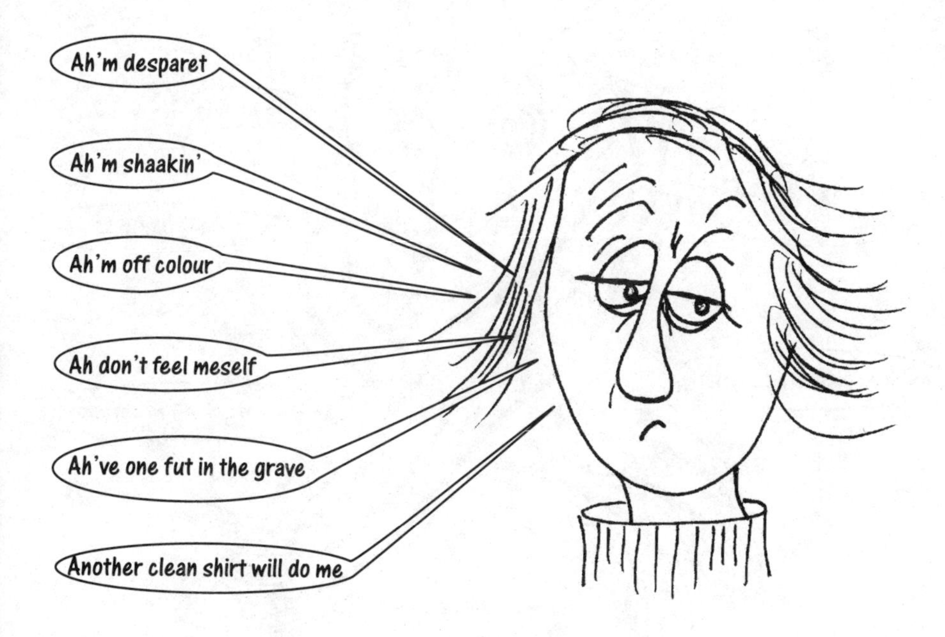

I feel that I have had too much alcohol

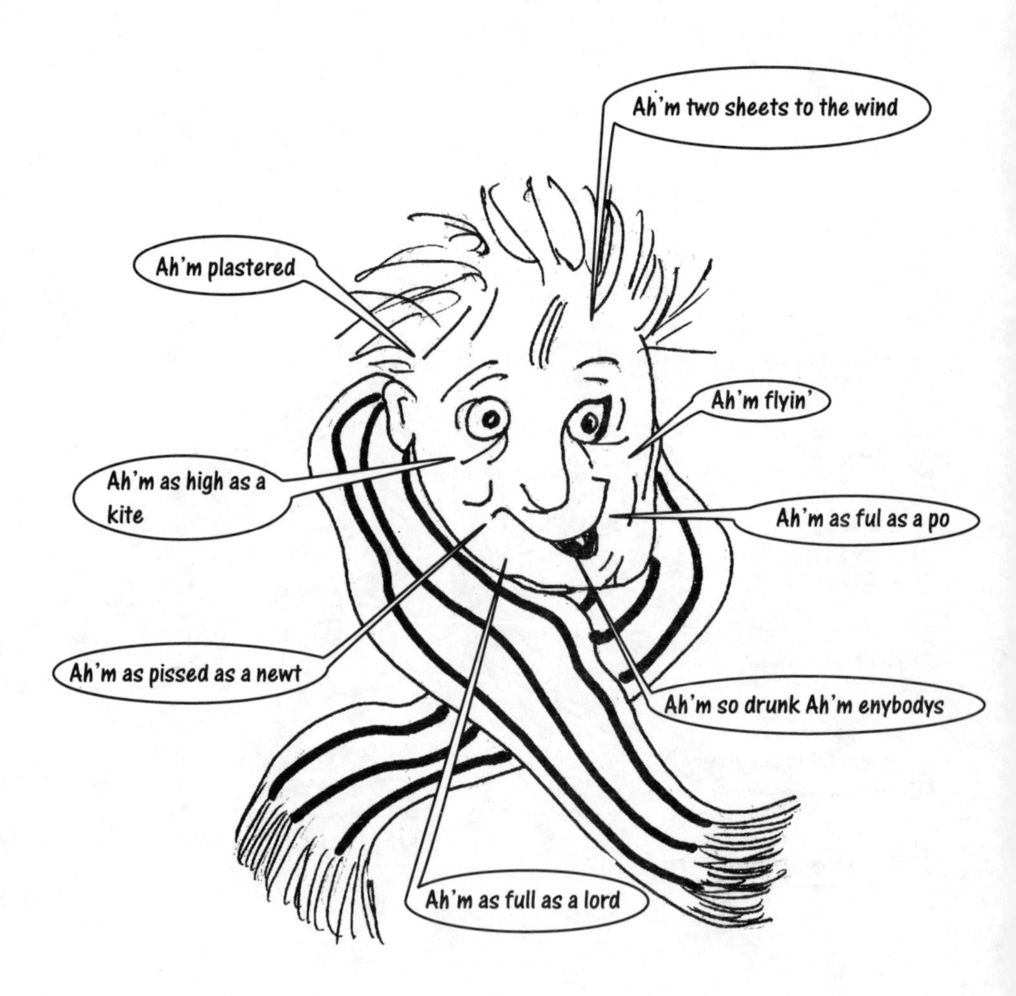

I am Hungry

Ah'm hunger's morr
Ah cud ate anything that ain't nailed down
Ah cud ate a pig's arse
Ah'm famished
Mah bally thinks mah throat's cut
Ah'm starvin' wif hunger

I need to visit the bathroom

I feel full of energy

I am angry

Ah'm as cross as two sticks
Ah'm full av piss an' wind
A'm laike two aul cyats wif thur tails tied
Ah'm laike two weasels in a bush

I feel frightened

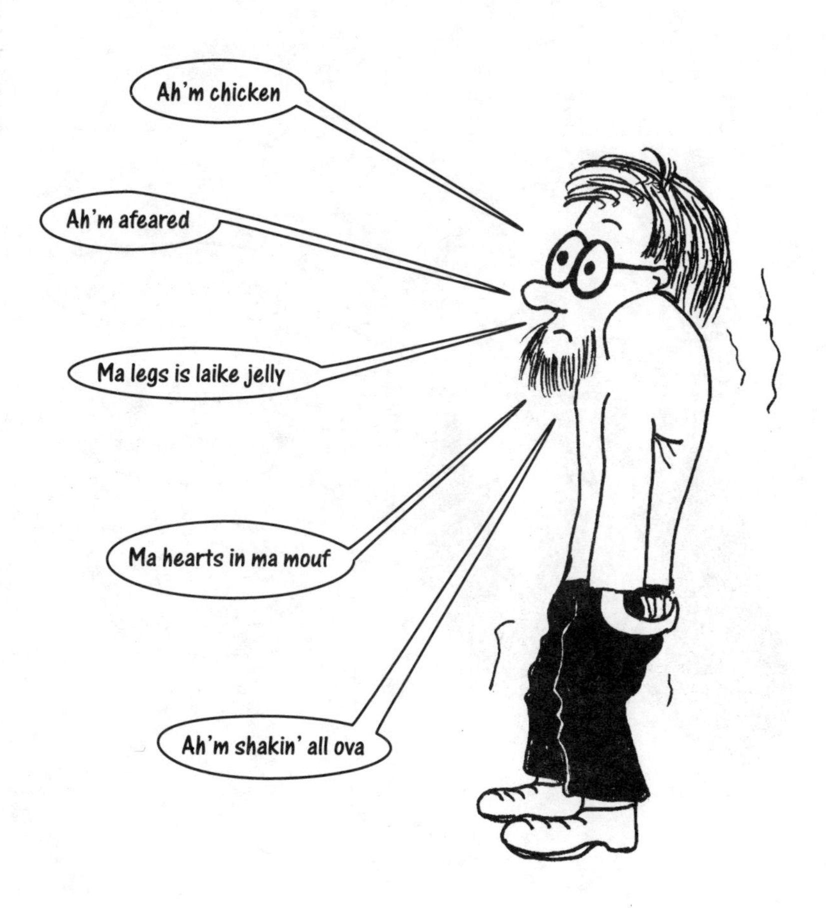

I feel very amused

I feel I have had enough to eat

Bare Nakit Woman - (Nude Female)

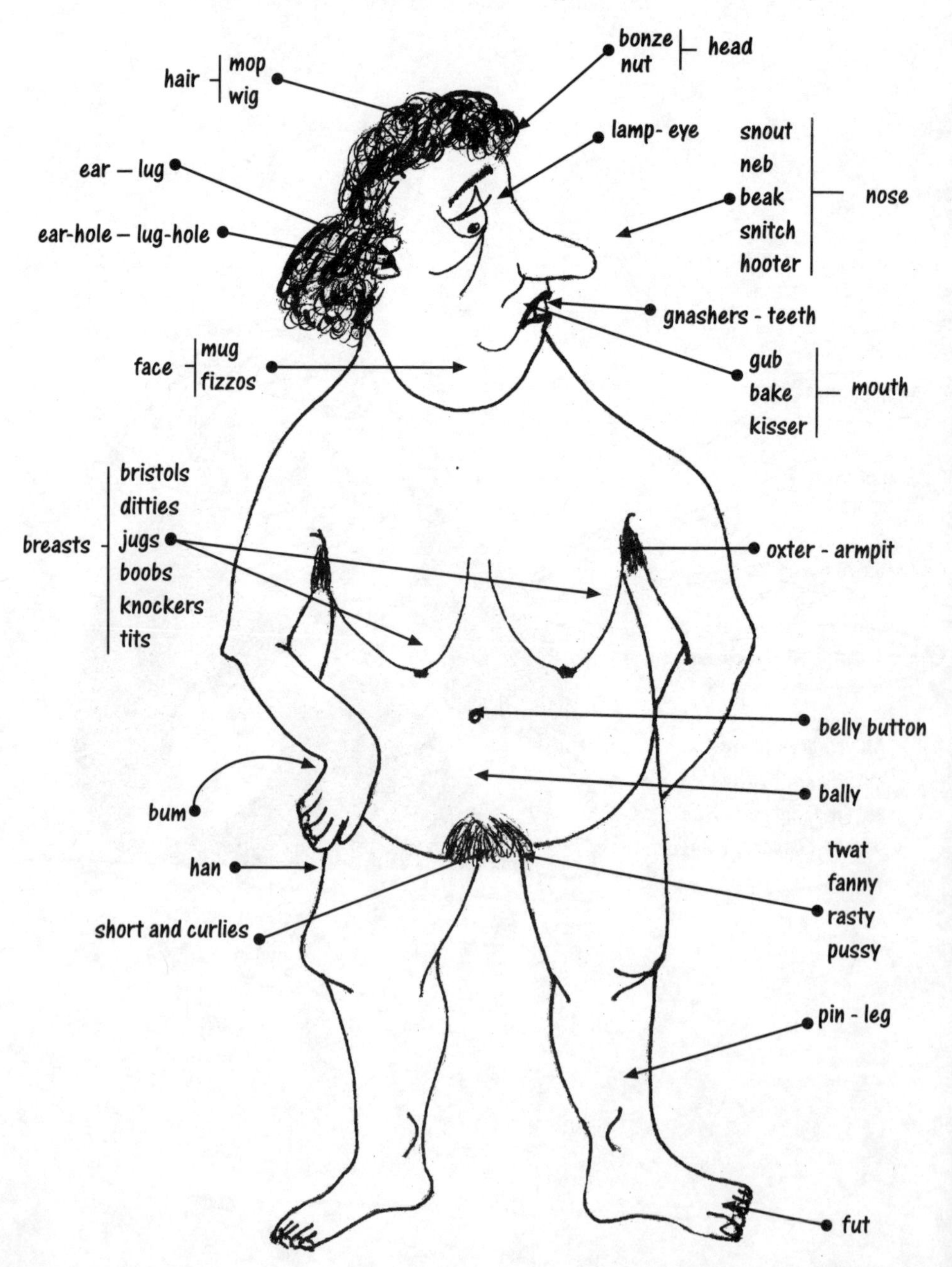

Bared Nakit Mon - (Nude Male)

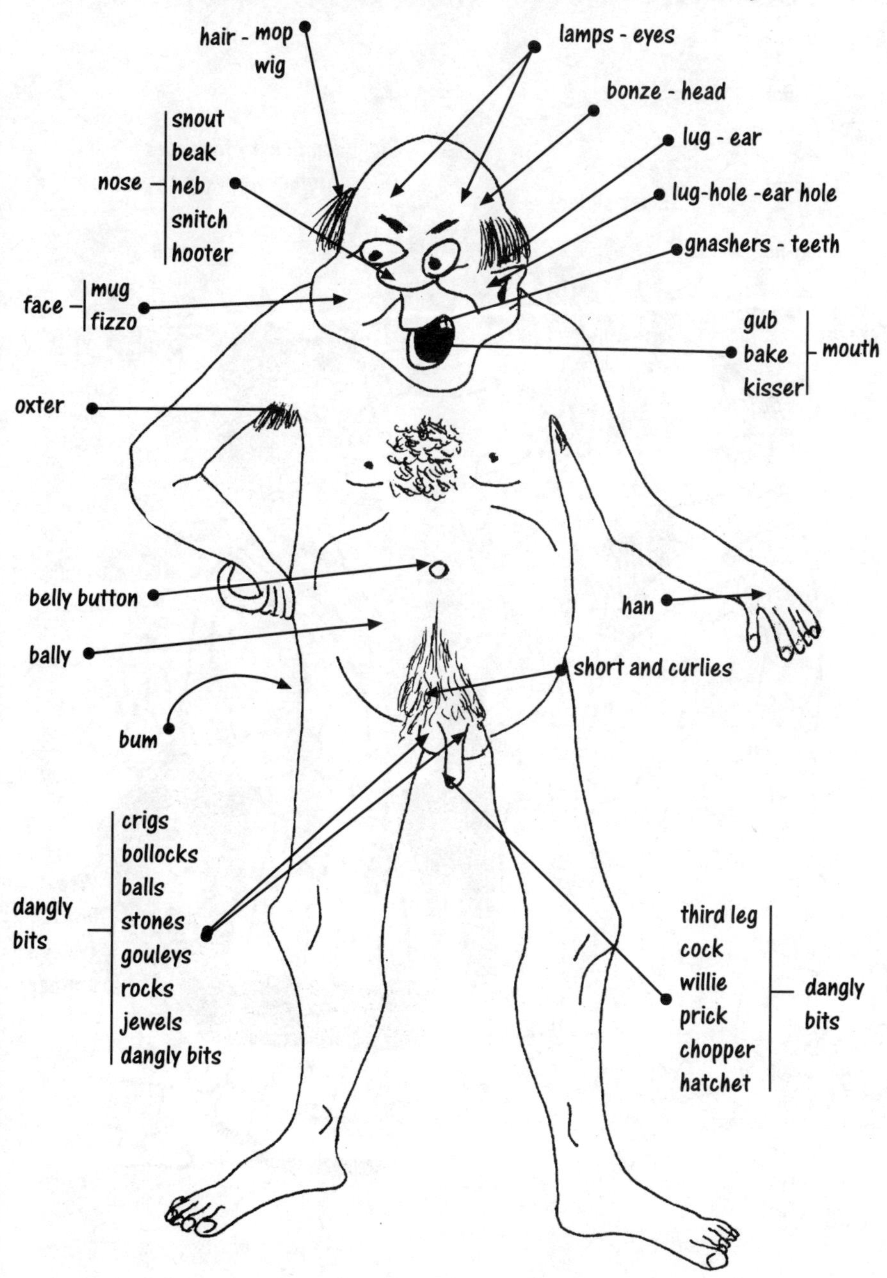

My Family

Big sister
(Elder sister)
Big brorr, Specky four eyes
(Elder brother who wears glasses)
Farr
(Father)
Morr
(Mother)
Wee
brorr
(younger
brother)
Cyat
(Cat)

More Members of my Family

My grand farr is a durty aul brute, he's pinching grandmorrs bum - (Grandfather is sexually harassing grandmother)

Out Shoppin' - (Going Shopping)

Out Fer A Bite – (Dining Out)

* a local delicacy

In Our Scullery – (In Our Kitchen)

Law and Order

Male/Female Relationships

Do ye think they'll click? –
(Will they find each other attractive and start dating)

Curtin - (Courtship)

Thur keepin company
Thur an item
Thur going together
Thur curtin
They've got a thing goin'

They have started dating

She fancies him - (She finds him attractive)
He's got the hots for her - (He lusts after her)

Making and Repelling Sexual Advances

1. We were petting

2. Your advances are unwelcome

Part Two:

Additional Vocabulary

Homework: Make sure you know all the vocabulary in Part One before proceeding further. Names of the parts of the body are particularly important.

Threats and Insults

Ulster is inhabited by friendly people who paradoxically have gained world renown for fighting. Perhaps the vigour of the vivid language used by the inhabitants is the cause? All the British Generals in World War Two had their roots in Ulster. Did they begin by being forced into self defence because their tongues led them into trouble? Who knows? The following phrases are to be used with care. They have been graded as an aid to avoiding or making trouble, depending on the requirements of the reader!

Insults Suggesting an Individual is Behaving Unwisely

(These insults apply to both men and women. For the sake of simplicity they have been written as applicable to men only.)

Luk at him! He shud join the circus!

They'll be takin' 'im awa in a straight-jacket!

He ain't operating wif the full deck!

He's two sandwhiches short of a picnic.

He's got a few tiles missin.'

He's off his skull.

He's off his nut!

He ain't right in the hed!

He's daaft.

He's outta hes mine.

He's off his nut!

Mild Threats with Affectionate Overtones

Phrase	Translation
give my head peace	*leave me alone*
yew'll put me away in the hed	*you are annoying me*
yew'd drive a body bananas	*you are irritating me*
yew'll put me in the looney bin	*you are driving me crazy*

Mild Threats to be Taken Seriously

Phrase	Translation
Wot are ye lukin' at? Want a photygraph?	*Why are you looking at me?*
Wots wrong wif yer bake?	*Why are you looking at me with that expression?*
I'll put my toe in ye.	*Stop annoying me.*
Clear awa arf.	*Go away.*
UFO	*Polite version: You go away.*

Serious Self-explanatory Threats

Watch out or yew'll be wearing yer tonsils as a moustache!

Watch yer face!

Ah'll re-arrange yer gub.

Are ye lukin' yer features re-arranged?

Ah'll kick yer spine up thru yer hat.

Ah'll bust yer bake! Ye pig ye!

Yer face is laike my bum!

Yew've a face laike a bag of spanners!

Ah'll knock ye into the middle av next week!

Ah'll swing fer ye! *(Literally: You are tempting me to murder you so I will be tried for murder and hung! Paradoxically this threat is not very serious!)*

Ah'll giv ye a good kick up the crigs!

Ye've a face only yer morr cud luv and even she had a hard time of it!

Ah'll swing fer ye!

Ah'll loss my toe in yer arse!

Yew've a mug I'd niver tire of kickin'!

Putting Snobs Down

Affectation is an attribute which is thoroughly disliked in Norn Iron.

Phrases Used to Show Disapproval of Snobbery

Phrase	Translation
They'd two sardines, be gad, an' they tole everybody they'd fish fur dinner.	*They were boasting.*
They think thur quare aul swanks.	*They think they are better than they are.*
Two sausages may hev rared yew but it niver rared me.	*My upbringing was superior.*
They've got esperayshuns beyond thur station.	*They have ideas beyond their means.*
They tok as if thur gubs wos full of marbles.	*Their manner of speech is affected.*

They'd two sardines, be gad, an' they tole everybody they'd fish fur dinner

Personal Comments

Fluent Norn Iron speakers are never lost for an aptly turned descriptive phrase about their fellow man. Use and enjoy!

Personal Comments Applicable to Men and Women

Phrase	Translation
Wot do ye expect from a pig but a grunt?	*Good behaviour cannot be expected from an ill-bred person.*
Yer futs mingin'.	*You have smelly feet.*
Yera wee git.	*You are a small unpleasant person.*
Yer backside's laike the back of a bus.	*You have a big bottom.*

Yera wee git

Yer as hard as a twenty minute egg.	*You lack compassion.*
Yer a hard lukin' ticket.	*You appear unsympathetic.*
Yer mug is laike the inside av a curren' loaf.	*You have a spotty complexion.*
Yew've a face laike a slap av fruitcake.	*You have a spotty complexion.*
Yer face is laike a well scalped arse.	*You have a ruddy complexion.*
One eye pointin' east the other west.	*Cross eyed.*
Yer smokin' laike a chimbley.	*You smoke too much.*
Yer gub's laike an ashcan.	*You smoke too much.*
They've been refeened by environment.	*They think they have gone up in the world.*
Yer gitting yersel rightly gathered.	*You are managing to collect a lot of material possessions.*
If wit wos shit ye'd be constipated.	*You are stupid.*
Yer quare an' gud at beatin' the gums.	*You are extremely good at arguing a point.*
Ye cud niver catch a peg in an entry wif thon legs.	*You are bow legged.*
Yer a right aule slap.	*You have had many (sexual) partners.*

Personal Comments Applicable to Women

Comment	Translation
Her arse luks as if it's chewing a carmel.	*She walks like Marilyn Monroe.*
Her knockers are so big she cud wear them as water wings.	*She has large breasts.*
She luks laike a pig wif lipstick.	*She is unattractive.*
Yera tough lukin' wee cuttie.	*You are a hard looking woman.*
She's the type av face ye'd not laike til wake next til.	*She is ugly.*
Her knockers are so big she cudn't fall flat on 'er face if she tried.	*She has large breasts.*

Her knockers are so big she cudn't fall flat on 'er face if she tried

Personal Comments Applicable to Men

He's built laike a brick shit house

Comment	Translation
He's well hung.	*He's a fine upstanding man.*
He alwus has a dew drop on the end of his nose.	*He's a drip.*
He's still wuring flures.	*He is unfashionable - literally - he is still wearing flared trousers.*
He's still dressed 70's style.	*His attire is unfashionable.*
His gub wud stop a bus at fifty yards.	*He has an ugly face.*
He's built laike a brick shit house.	*He is a hefty individual.*

Thur Tight

In Norn Iron thrift is a quality which is admired while being mean is despised. The ideal is to manage one's affairs so well that it is possible to give money to charity and to be very hospitable. The Province has an excellent record in helping the less fortunate and strangers are, as long as they like the place, made very welcome. To describe someone as mean suggests great disapproval and dislike. The local word for mean is TIGHT. This is confusing as 'tight' can also mean has consumed too much alcohol.

The following phrases suggest meanness.

Thur as tight as a sheep's arse in a hail storm.

Thur as tight as a pig's arse in a rainstorm.

Thur so tight they'd use a straw to suck moisture off a cow's arse through a hedge.

Thur that tight they'd skin a fart

Thur that tight they'd skin a fart.

Thur as tight as a duck's arse.

Thur as tight as a shark's arse at 50 fathoms.

Thur as tight as a fish's arse and that's water tight.

Thur as tight as a donkey's arse pullin' a load goin' up hill.

Thur that tight they wudn't give ye the steam of thur pee.

In Sickness and Health

If you suspect someone is unwell a suitable phrase to use is 'You all right, luv?', meaning 'Are you feeling alright?'

If you feel someone is running a temperature and looks flushed say:

'Yer orful rosy lukin'

or

Yer cheeks are laike two wee apples.

'You all right, luv?'

The act of vomiting is unpleasant and memorable. Local powers of description have resulted in the development of the following phrases meaning 'to vomit'. They may be used for either males or females:

He wus sick out loud.

She wus tho'ing up rings roun' her.

She wus bokin' rings roun' her.

He wus calling for Shuey down the big white telephone.

He wus as sick as a dog.

She wus lashin' rings.

Suitable Phrases to Denote that Someone Looks Very Ill

yer a shaakin' colour

yer the worst case Ah ever saw

yer brutal lukin'

Ye luk awful. Ye've got such black rings under yer eyes they luk laike two pissholes in the snow.

Ah feel it's an orful pity orf ye

Ye luk as if ye've been in the grave fur a week

Ye luk laike corn beef

Yer the worst case Ah ever saw

Complaints Requiring Medical Attention

Ah haf to go til the big dacter

Phrase	Translation
Ah haf to go til the big dacter.	*I need to attend the doctor.*
Ah wus in bed wif the dacter.	*I had to call the doctor and request a home visit.*
They didn't know wot to do wif me in that 'ospital.	*The specialist was puzzled by my symptoms.*
He's awful bad in the 'ospital.	*He's very ill in hospital.*
He had tubes everywhur.	*He was on life support.*
He wos in entensive cur.	*He was in the intensive care unit.*
He had hoses coming out of his nose.	*He was on life support.*
She's in fur a hysterical rectum.	*She is undergoing a hysterectomy.*

Ah wos in bed with my kidneys

Specific Complaints

Phrase	Translation
lisen til her barkin'	*she is displaying a bad cough*
she's bad wif 'er hed	*she has a headache*
she's got 'er death	*she has a bad cold*
it wos a quhange lump	*a suspicious lump*
her feet's beelin'	*her feet are either supturating or she has a blister*
Ah wos in bed with my kidneys	*I was confined to bed with a kidney complaint*
she got a dose of the runs	*she had diarrhoea*
'er lamps is bad	*she has poor eyesight*
he's mutton jeff	*he is deaf*
she colopsed	*she collapsed*
quit it ye, or ye'll smit me	*stop coughing (or sneezing) in case you infect me*
Ah've an absect up me oxters	*I have an abscess in my armpit*
she shudn't have went for her 'flu shot	*being immunised against influenza was unwise*
Ah need physio the rapist	*I need a physiotherapist*
Ah'm turrible bad wif me stomick	*I am experiencing stomach trouble*
Ah'm bad wif me back	*I have backache*
Ah wus high styrickal	*I suffered an attack of hysterics*

Feeling Nervous

If you are feeling nervous because you have been unwise and are frightened of being caught, or you are facing some sort of ordeal, such as a big interview, the correct term is 'Ah wos shittin' bricks!'

Feelings which may be engendered by the female (or male) menopause, may be expressed as 'Ah wos bad wif my nerves.'

He's a moon man

There are a number of sayings to describe people who appear to be a bit silly and are acting unwisely, such as:

'He's away wif the fairies.'

'He's a moon man.'

'He's a right looney.'

'He shud be in the looney bin.'*

'He shud be in the funny farm.'*

'He's livin' on the edge.'

'He's awa' in the hed.'

'He's certifiable.'

'He's lost his marleys.'

*Hospital which attends to mental disease.

The above statements may be used to denote either males or females. For the sake of simplicity they have been written to indicate males.

Suffering From Severe Mental Illness

There are several correct ways of saying that an individual has become so mentally deranged that the services of either a psychologist or a psychiatrist have been sought, namely:

He had til see a trick cyclist.

He went til see a head shrink.

He lost his marleys an' had til go an' see one of them dacters.

Sick of Looking at Pictures and Wanting to Get Down to Some Serious Grammar?

When learning any new language it is helpful to master a few rules of grammar. It is impossible to speak like a native without using the correct structure. Serious students should learn how to conjugate the verb to laike (like). Having mastered this basic conjugation it is then possible to apply it to other verbs.

The verb LAIKE meaning LIKE

Ah laike	(I like)	wees laike	(we like)
yew laike	(you like)	youse laike	(you like)
he/she laikes	(he/she likes)	them ones laike	(they like)